IN HIM WILL I TRUST

A Boy's Account of his Captivity
among the American Indians
1689

MORE TITLES AVAILABLE FROM PSALM 78 MINISTRIES

Call Me No Hero

Coachman to the King

Daybreak in Alaska

Dangerous Endeavor: The Tale of the Lewis and Clark Expedition

*Driven to Resistance: A History of the Revolutionary War,
as told by those who lived it*

Invisible Hero

I Want to Catch a Dinosaur

John Paton for Young Folks

Just Jim: A Little Boy, a Time of Trouble, and a Faithful God

New Testament Greek for the Beginner

Pierre Viret: the Angel of the Reformation

Pirates, Puritans, and the Perils of the High Seas

Tremble: A Child's First Book on Space

Where is Wisdom? Where did God Hide It?

With God in the Wilderness

Without a Home or Country: A Stirring Tale of the Confederate Navy

Words of the Wise

For a full listing of titles, please visit: psalm78ministries.com

IN HIM WILL I TRUST

A Boy's Account of his Captivity
among the American Indians
1689

JOHN GYLES

A tale of God's Providence and Mercy
through Hardship and Suffering

EDITED BY GENEVIEVE SHEATS

In Him Will I Trust: A Boy's Account of his Captivity among the American Indains

Originally published under the title:
Memoirs of Odd Adventures and Signal Deliverances in the Captivity of John Gyles, Esq. (Boston, 1736)

Copyright © 2013 Genevieve Sheats

All rights reserved.
No part of this publication may be reproduced or distributed in any form or by any means, without written consent from the publisher.

Second printing, 2019

Published by:

Psalm 78 Ministries
P. O. Box 950
Monticello, FL 32345
www.psalm78ministries.com

Printed in the United States of America.

ISBN: 978-1-938822-33-9

Scripture quotations are taken from the King James Version of the Holy Scriptures. Divine pronouns have been capitalized.

Psalm 91

He that dwelleth in the secret place of the most High
shall abide under the shadow of the Almighty.
I will say of the Lord, He is my refuge and
my fortress: my God; in Him will I trust.

Surely He shall deliver thee from the snare of the fowler,
and from the noisome pestilence.
He shall cover thee with His feathers,
and under His wings shalt thou trust:
His truth shall be thy shield and buckler.
Thou shalt not be afraid for the terror by night;
nor for the arrow that flieth by day;
nor for the pestilence that walketh in darkness;
nor for the destruction that wasteth at noonday.

A thousand shall fall at thy side, and ten thousand
at thy right hand; but it shall not come nigh thee.
Only with thine eyes shalt thou behold and see
the reward of the wicked. Because thou hast made the Lord,
which is my refuge, even the most High,
thy habitation; there shall no evil befall thee,
neither shall any plague come nigh thy dwelling.

For He shall give His angels charge over thee,
to keep thee in all thy ways. They shall bear thee up
in their hands, lest thou dash thy foot against a stone.
Thou shalt tread upon the lion and adder:
the young lion and the dragon shalt thou trample under feet.

Because he hath set his love upon Me,
therefore will I deliver him:
I will set him on high, because he hath known My name.
He shall call upon Me, and I will answer him:
I will be with him in trouble; I will deliver him,
and honour him. With long life will I satisfy him,
and shew him My salvation.

(1)

MEMOIRS
Of Odd Adventures and Signal Deliverances in the Captivity of

John Gyles, Esq;

CHAP. I.
Containing the Occurrences of the first Year.

SECT. I. Of the taking the Family of Thomas Gyles, Esq;

ON the second Day of *August*, Anno *Christi* 1689, in the Morning, my honoured Father *Thomas Gyles*, Esq; went with some Labourers, my two Elder Brothers and my self, to one of his Farms, which lay on the River about three Miles above *Fort-Charles* †, adjoining to *Pemmaquid Falls*; there to gather in his English Harvest, and laboured securely till Noon. But after we had Dined, our People went to their Labour, some in one Field to their English Hay, the others to another

---

† *Fort-Charles* stood on the Spot where *Frederick's-Fort* was, not long since, founded the Hon. Col. DUNBAR: The Township adjoining thereto was called *James-Town*, in honour to the Duke of *York*: In this Town within a quarter of a Mile of the Fort was the Dwelling House of *Thomas Gyles*, Esq; from which he went out that unhappy Morning.

B   Field

Title page of the 1736 edition

TABLE OF CONTENTS

Introduction 11

A Note on the Text 13

1 My Capture by Indians 15

2 My Coming to an Indian Village 29

3 Miraculously Preserved 43

4 Further Difficulties and Deliverances 55

5 The Lord's Protecting Me from Harm 63

6 The Indians Calling upon the Devil 71

7 Sold to the French 77

8 My Trial with False Religion 87

9 God's Mercy in Returning Me to the English 91

Introduction

The history of John Gyles is a vivid account of a young boy's life as a captive among the savage North American Indians. Trials, hardships, death, and suffering are painted with broad strokes across nearly nine years of Gyles' boyhood days. Taken captive at about ten years of age, facing the loss of parents, siblings, and dearest friends, and though surrounded by the darkness of demon worship and savage brutality, the tale of Gyles' life is a tale of hope, of trust, and of an unending vision of the goodness of God amidst some of the most harrowing times imaginable.

What is the contemporary reader to learn from this seventeenth-century story of Indian attacks, murders, and tragedies? In Gyles' own words, he penned this little book in order "that we might have a memento ever ready at hand to excite in ourselves gratitude and thankfulness to God" for His goodness, mercy, and unfailing love to His undeserving children.

May Gyles' wish be fulfilled in the republication of this work, and may the reading of it cause a new generation to ponder afresh the faithfulness and goodness of their God, and acknowledge their full dependence on, and undying gratitude to, our Lord and Savior Jesus Christ.

— R. A. Sheats

A Note on the Text

The text of *In Him Will I Trust* is an abridged copy of the first edition of John Gyles' autobiography, originally published in 1736.

Though faithfulness to the original text has been strictly maintained, it has been deemed prudent to conform spelling, capitalization, and punctuation to modern standards. Chapter breaks have been added to ease reading, and footnoted definitions of archaic or lesser-known words have been included to facilitate comprehension. Study questions and Scripture verses have also been added to each chapter.

Because Gyles' account deals mainly with life among the American Indians, some passages of the book may be disturbing to younger readers. It is therefore advised that parents preview the volume prior to reading aloud as a family.

CHAPTER ONE

My Capture by Indians

"He that dwelleth in the secret place of the most High shall abide under the Shadow of the Almighty. I will say of the LORD, *He is my refuge and my fortress: my God; in Him will I trust."*
Psalm 91:1–2

On the second day of August, in the year of our Lord 1689, in the morning, my honored father, Thomas Gyles, Esq., went with some laborers, my two elder brothers and myself, to one of his farms, which laid upon the river about three miles above Fort Charles, adjoining to Pemaquid Falls,[1] there to gather in his English harvest, and we labored securely till noon.

But after we had dined, our people went to their labor, some in one field to their English hay, the others to another field of English corn. My father, the youngest of my two brothers, and myself, tarried near to the farm-house in which we had dined till about one of the clock, when we heard the report[2] of several great guns from the fort. Upon the hearing

---
[1] **Pemaquid Falls** – south coast of Maine

[2] **report** – sound

of them my father said that he hoped it was a signal of good news, and [hoped] that the great council had sent back the soldiers to cover[3] the inhabitants.

But, to our great surprise, about thirty or forty Indians discharged a volley of shot at us from behind a rising ground near our barn. The yelling of the Indians, the whistling of their shot, and the voice of my father, whom I heard cry out, "What now! What now!" so terrified me, though he seemed to be handling a gun, that I endeavored to make my escape. My brother ran one way and I another, and looking over my shoulder I saw a stout fellow, painted, pursuing me with a gun, and a cutlass glittering in his hand, which I expected every moment in my brains. I presently fell down, and the Indian took me by the left hand, offered me no abuse, but seized[4] my arms, lift me up, and pointed to the place where the people were at work about the hay, and led me that way.

As we passed, we crossed my father, who looked very pale and bloody, and walked very slowly. When we came to the place, I saw two men shot down on the flats.[5] There the Indians brought two captives, one man and my brother James (he that

---

[3] **cover** – protect
[4] **seized** – tied
[5] **flats** – low ground

endeavored to escape by running from the house when I did).

After they had done what mischief they could, [the Indians] sat down, making us sit with them. And, after some time arose, pointed to us to go eastward. They marched about a quarter of a mile and then made a halt, and brought my father to us.

My father replied that he was a dying man, and wanted no favor of them but to pray with his children. Which, being granted, he recommended[6] us to the protection and blessing of God Almighty, then gave us the best advice, and took his leave for this life, hoping in God that we should meet in a better. He parted with a cheerful voice, but looked very pale by reason of his great loss of blood, which boiled out of his shoes. The Indians led him aside and killed him. (I afterward heard that he had five or seven shot-holes through his waistcoat or jacket, and that the Indians covered him with some boughs.)

The Indians led us, their captives, on the east side of the river towards the fort, and when we came within a mile and half of the fort and town, and could see the fort, we saw firing and smoke on all sides. Here we made a short stop, and then we moved within or near the distance of three-quarters of a mile from the fort into a thick swamp.

There I saw my mother and <u>my two little sisters</u>, and many other

[6] **recommended** – committed with prayer

captives taken from the town. My mother asked me of my father. I told her that he was killed, but could say no more for grief. She burst into tears, and the Indians moved me a little farther off and tied me to a tree.

The Indians came to New Harbor[7] and sent spies several days to observe how and where the people were employed, etc., who found that the men were generally at work at noon, and left about their houses only women and children. Therefore the Indians divided themselves into several parties, some ambushing the way between the fort and the houses, [and some] likewise between them and the distant fields. And then, alarming the farthest off first, they killed and took the people as they moved toward the town and fort, at their pleasure, so that very few escaped to the fort.

On the first stir about the fort my youngest brother was at play near the same, and ran in, and so by God's goodness was preserved.

Captain Weems[8] with great courage and resolution, defended the weak old fort two days till that he was much wounded, and the best of his men killed, and then beat for a parley,[9] and the conditions were:

---

[7] **New Harbor** – about 3 miles from Pemaquid
[8] **Captain Weems** – commander of the fort
[9] **parley** – negotiation

1. That they, the Indians, should give him Mr. Poteshall's sloop.[10]

2. That they should not molest him in carrying off the few people that had got into the fort, and three captives that they had taken.

3. That the English should carry off in their hands what they could from the fort.

On these conditions the fort was surrendered, and Captain Weems went off; and soon after the Indians set on fire the fort and houses, which made a terrible blast, and was a melancholy sight to us poor captives, who were sad spectators!

After the Indians had thus laid waste Pemaquid, they moved us all to New Harbor. And when we turned our backs on the town, my heart was ready to break! I saw my mother. She spoke to me, but I could not answer her! That night we tarried at New Harbor, and the next day went in their canoes for Penobscot.

About noon, the canoe which my mother, and that which I was in, came side by side, whether accidentally or by my mother's desire[11] I cannot say. She asked me how I did. I think I said "Pretty well," (though my heart was full of grief). Then she said, "Oh my child! how joyful and pleasant would it be if we were going to old England, to see your uncle Chalker and other friends there. Poor babe! We are going into the wilderness, the Lord knows where!" She burst into tears, and the canoes parted! That night following, the Indians with their captives lodged on an

---

[10] **sloop** – a sailing vessel with one mast
[11] **desire** – request

island.

A few days after we arrived at Penobscot Fort, where I again saw my mother, my brother and sisters, and many other captives. I think we tarried here eight days. And in that time the Jesuit[12] had a great mind to buy me. My Indian master made a visit to the Jesuit, and carried me with him. I saw the Jesuit show him pieces of gold, and understood afterward that he tendered them for me. The Jesuit gave me a biscuit, which I put into my pocket, and dare not eat, but buried it under a log, fearing that he had put something in it to make me love him, for I was very young, and had heard much of the Papists torturing the Protestants, etc., so that I hated the sight of a Jesuit.

When my mother heard the talk of my being sold to a Jesuit, she said to me, "Oh, my dear child! if it were God's will, I had rather follow you to your grave, or never see you more in this world, than you should be sold to a Jesuit, for a Jesuit will ruin you, body and soul!"

And it pleased God to grant her request, for she never saw me more! Though she and my two little sisters were, after several years' captivity, redeemed, she died before I returned. And my brother, who was taken with me, was, after several

---

[12] **Jesuit** – a member of the Society of Jesus, a Roman Catholic order

years' captivity, most barbarously murdered by the Indians.

My Indian master carried me up Penobscot river to a village called Madawamkee, which stands on a point of land between the main river and a branch which heads to the east of it. At home I had ever seen strangers treated with the utmost civility, and, being a stranger, I expected some kind treatment here, but soon found myself deceived, for I presently saw a number of squaws[13] got together in a circle, dancing and yelling. And an old grimace–squaw took me by the hand, and led me to the ring, where the other squaws seized me by the hair of my head, and by my hands and feet, like so many furies,[14] but my Indian master presently laid down a pledge and released me.

A captive among the Indians is exposed to all manner of abuse unless his master, or some of his master's relations, lay down a ransom, such as a bag of corn, or a blanket, or such like, by which they may redeem them from their cruelties for that dance, so that he shall not be touched by any.

---

[13] **squaws** – Indian women

[14] **furies** – wicked and violent goddesses

"He that dwelleth in the secret place of the most High shall abide under the Shadow of the Almighty. I will say of the LORD, He is my refuge and my fortress: my God; in Him will I trust."
Psalm 91:1–2

Questions for Comprehension and Discussion

1. How was John Gyles captured by the Indians?

2. What was Gyles' father's final act before he died?

3. What became of the English fort?

4. Who did Gyles' mother perceive to be a worse enemy than the Indians? Why?

5. How did Gyles expect to be treated as a stranger in the Indians' dwelling?

6. What is the Biblical response to man-stealing and murder?

7. List Scriptures that instruct us how to treat strangers.

CHAPTER TWO

My Coming to an Indian Village

"He shall call upon Me, and I will answer him: I will be with him in trouble; I will deliver him, and honour him."
Psalm 91:15

The next day we went up that eastern branch of Penobscot River many leagues, carried[1] over land to a large pond, and from one pond to another, till, in a few days, we went down a river which vents itself into St. John's River. But, before we came to the mouth of this river, we carried[1] over a long carrying place to Medocktack Fort, which stands on a bank of St. John's River.

My Indian master went before, and left me with an old Indian and two or three squaws. The old man often said (which was all the English that he could speak), "By and by[2] come to a great town and fort." So that I comforted myself in thinking how finely I should be refreshed, etc., when I came to this great town.

---

[1] **carried** – transported boats or canoes
[2] **by and by** – soon

After some miles' travel we came in sight of a large cornfield, and soon after [saw] the fort, to my great surprise. For two or three squaws met us, took off my pack, and led me to a large hut or wigwam, where thirty or forty Indians were dancing and yelling round five or six poor captives, who had been taken some months before from Quochech, at the same time when Major Waldron was most barbarously butchered by them. I was whirled in among them, and we looked on each other with a sorrowful countenance. And presently one of them was seized by each hand and foot by four Indians, who mistreated him terribly.

The Indians looked on me with a fierce countenance, signifying that it would be my turn next. They champed[3] cornstalks, and threw them in my hat which was in my hand. I smiled on them, though my heart ached. I looked on one and another, but could not perceive that any eye pitied me.

Presently came a squaw and a little girl, and laid down a bag of corn in the ring. The little girl took me by the hand, making signs for me to go out of the circle with them. But, not knowing their custom, I supposed that they designed to kill me, and would not go out with them. Then a grave Indian came and gave me a short pipe, and said in English, "Smoke it." then took me by the hand and led me out. But my heart ached, thinking

---

[3] **champed** – chewed

myself near my end. But he carried me to a French hut about a mile from the Indian fort.

The Frenchman was not at home, but his wife, who was a squaw, had some discourse with my Indian friend, which I did not understand. We tarried about two hours and returned to the village, where they gave me some victuals.[4] Not long after I saw one of my fellow-captives, who gave me a melancholy account of their sufferings after I left them.

After some weeks had passed, we left the village and went up St. John's River about ten miles to a branch called Medockscenecasis, where there was one wigwam. At our arrival an old squaw saluted me with a yell, taking me by the hair and

---

[4] **victuals** – food

one hand, but I was so rude as to break her hold and quit[5] myself. She gave me a filthy grin, and the Indians set up a laugh, so it passed over. Here we lived upon fish, wild grapes, roots, etc., which was hard living to me.

When the winter came on we went up the river till the ice came down and ran thick in the river, and then, according to the Indian custom, laid up our canoes till the spring. And then we traveled sometimes on the ice, and sometimes on the land till we came to a river that was open, and not fordable, where we made a raft and passed over, bag and baggage. I met with no abuse from them in this winter's hunting, though I was put to great hardships in carrying burdens and for want[6] of food. For they underwent the same difficulty, and would often encourage me, saying in broken English, "By and by[7] great deal moose." But they could not answer any question that I asked them. So that, knowing nothing of their customs and way of life, though I thought it tedious to be constantly moving from place to place, yet it might be in some respects an advantage. For it ran still in my mind that we were traveling to some settlement, and when my burden was over-heavy and the Indians left me behind, and the still evening came on, I fancied I could see through the bushes and hear the people of some great town, which hope might be some support to me in the day, though I found not the town at night.

Thus we have been hunting three hundred miles from the sea, and knew [of] no man within fifty or sixty miles of us. We were eight or ten in number, and had but two Indian men with guns, on whom we wholly depended for food. And if any disaster had happened, we must all have perished. And sometimes we had no manner of sustenance for three or four days, but God wonderfully provides for all creatures! In one of those fasts God's providence was remarkable. Our two Indian men, in hunting, started[8] a moose, there being a shallow crusted snow on

---

[5] **quit** – free
[6] **want** – lack
[7] **by and by** – soon
[8] **started** – startled

the ground. But the moose discovered them, and ran with great force into a swamp. The Indians went round the swamp, and finding no track, returned at night to the wigwam and told what had happened.

The next morning they followed him on the track and soon found the moose lying on the snow, for, crossing the roots of a large tree that had been blown up by the roots (having ice underneath), the moose in his furious flight broke through and hitched[9] one of his hind legs in among the roots so fast[10] that by striving to get it out, he pulled the thigh-bone out of the socket at the hip. Thus extraordinarily were we provided for in our great strait.[11] And then we feasted.

And an old squaw and captive, if any present, must stand without the wigwam, shaking their hands and body, as in a dance,

---

[9] **hitched** – entangled
[10] **fast** – firmly
[11] **strait** – difficulty

and singing, "Wegage oh nelo who!" which if Englished[12] would be, "Fat is my eating." This is to signify their thankfulness in feasting times! And when this was spent, we fasted till further success.

    We moved still further up the country after moose when our store was out, so that by the spring we had got to the northward of the Lady Mountains. And when the spring came on and the rivers broke up, we moved back to the head of St. John's River, and there made canoes of moose hides, sewing three or four together and pitching[13] the seams with charcoal beaten and mixed with balsam.[14] Then we went down the river to a place called Madawescok. There an old man lived and kept a sort of trading-house, where we tarried several days, and went farther down the river till we came to the greatest falls in these parts, called Checanekepeag, where we carried[15] a little way over the land and, putting off our canoes, we went downstream still. And as we passed down by the mouth of any large branches, we saw Indians, but when any dance was proposed, I was bought off.

---

[12] **Englished** – translated into English
[13] **pitching** – smearing with pitch
[14] **balsam** – resin or sap
[15] **carried** – transported boats or canoes

At length we arrived at the place where we left our birch canoes in the fall, and put our baggage into them, and went in them down to the fort.

There we planted corn, and after planting went a–fishing and to look for and dig roots till the corn was fit to weed. And after weeding, [we] took a second tour on the same errand, and returned to hill our corn. And after hilling[16] we went some distance from the fort and field up the river to take salmon and other fish and dry them for food, till corn was filled with the milk, some of which we dried then, the other as it ripened.

Thus God wonderfully favored me and carried me through the first year of my captivity.

---

[16] **hilling** – raising dirt around plants

"He shall call upon Me, and I will answer him: I will be with him in trouble; I will deliver him, and honour him."
Psalm 91:15

Questions for Comprehension and Discussion

1. What was Gyles' reception at the Indian village?

2. List some of the ways God protected Gyles during his stay at the village.

3. How did Gyles spend the winter?

4. How did God provide food for the hunting party?

5. To what does Gyles ascribe his surviving the first year of his captivity?

6. Using Scripture, list some reasons why God honors and delivers His children from danger and trials.

CHAPTER THREE

Miraculously Preserved

"A thousand shall fall at thy side, and ten thousand at thy right hand; but it shall not come nigh thee."
Psalm 91:7

When any great number of Indians meet, or when any captives have been lately taken, or when any captives desert and are retaken, the Indians have a dance, and at these dances they mistreat the unhappy people who fall into their hands. My unfortunate brother who was taken with me, after about three years' captivity, deserted with an Englishman who was taken from Casco Bay, and was retaken by the Indians at New Harbor, and carried back to Penobscot Fort, where they were both tortured at a stake by fire for some time. Thus they divert[1] themselves in their dances!

On the second spring of my captivity my Indian master and his squaw went to Canada, but sent me down the river with several Indians to the fort in order to plant corn. The day before we came to the planting field we met two young Indian men who seemed to be in great haste. After they had passed us

---
[1] **divert** – amuse

I understood that they were going with an express to Canada, and that there was an English vessel at the mouth of the river. I not perfect in the language, nor knowing that English vessels traded with them in time of war, supposed a peace was concluded on, and that the captives would be released, and was so transported[2] with the fancy[3] that I slept but little (if at all) that night.

Early the next morning we came to the village, where the ecstasy ended; for I had no sooner landed, but three or four Indians dragged me to the great wigwam where they were yelling and dancing round James Alexander, a Jersey man, who was taken from Falmouth in Casco Bay. This was occasioned by two families of Cape Sable Indians who, having lost some friends by a number of English fishermen, came some hundreds of miles to revenge themselves on the poor captives! They soon came to me and mistreated me, and then threw me into the ring to my fellow captive, and took him out again and repeated their barbarities to him. And then I was hauled out again by three Indians by the hair of my head, and held down by it till one beat me on the back and shoulders so long that my breath was almost beat out of my body. And then others put a tomahawk into my hand, and ordered me get up and dance and sing Indian, which I performed with the greatest reluctance, and in the act seemed resolute to purchase my death by killing two or three of those monsters of cruelty, thinking it impossible to survive their bloody treatment. But it was impressed on my mind, "Tis not in their power to take away your life," so I desisted.

Then those Cape Sable Indians came to me again like bears bereaved of their whelps, saying, "Shall we who have lost relations[4] by the English suffer[5] an English voice to be heard among us?" etc. Then they beat me again with the axe. Then I

---

[2] **transported** – enraptured
[3] **fancy** – thought
[4] **relations** – relatives
[5] **suffer** – allow

repented that I had not sent two or three of them out of the world before me, for I thought I had much rather die than suffer any longer.

They left me the second time, and the other Indians put the tomahawk into my hand again and compelled me to sing. And then I seemed more resolute than before to destroy some of them, but a strange and strong impulse that I should return to my own place and people suppressed it as often as such a motion rose in my breast. Not one of the Indians showed the least compassion, but I saw the tears run down plentifully on the cheeks of a Frenchman that sat behind, which did not alleviate the tortures that poor James and I were forced to endure for the most part of this tedious day, for they were continued till the evening, and were the most severe that ever I met with in the whole six years that I was captive with the Indians.

After they had thus inhumanly abused us, two Indians took us up and threw us out of the wigwam, and we crawled away on our hands and knees, and were scarce able to walk for several days. Some time after they again concluded on a merry dance when I was at some distance from the wigwam dressing leather, and an Indian was so kind as to tell me that they had got James Alexander, and were in search for me. My Indian master and his squaw bid me run as for my life into a swamp and hide, and not to discover[6] myself unless they both came to me, for

---
[6] **discover** – reveal

then I might be assured the dance was over. I was now master of their language, and a word or a wink was enough to excite me to take care of one. I ran to the swamp and hid in the thickest place that I could find. I heard hallooing and whooping all around me. Sometimes they passed very near and I could hear some threaten and others flatter me, but I was not disposed to dance. And if they had come upon me, I resolved to show them a pair of heels, and they must have had good luck to have catched me.

I heard no more of them till about evening, for I think I slept, when they came again, calling, "Chon, Chon," but John would not trust them. After they were gone, my master and his squaw came where they told me to hide, but could not find me. And when I heard them say, with some concern, that they believed that the other Indians had frightened me into the woods and that I was lost, I came out, and they seemed well pleased. And [they] told me that James had had a bad day of it; that as soon as he was released he ran away into the woods, and they believed he was gone to the Mohawks.[7]

James soon returned and gave me a melancholy account of his sufferings, and the Indians' fright concerning the Mohawks passed over. They often had terrible apprehensions of the incursions[8] of the Mohawks.

One very hot season a great number gathered together at the village, and being a very droughty[9] people, they kept James and myself night and day fetching water from a cold spring that ran out of a rocky hill about three-quarters of a mile from the fort. In going thither we crossed a large interval cornfield, and then a descent to a lower interval before we ascended the hill to the spring. James being almost dead, as well as I, with this continual fatigue, contrived to fright the Indians. He told me of it, but conjured me to secrecy, yet said he knew that I could keep counsel.

The next dark night, James, going for water, set his kettle on the descent to the lowest interval, and ran back to the fort, puffing and blowing as in the utmost surprise, and told

---

[7] **Mohawks** – an Indian tribe

[8] **incursions** – attacks

[9] **droughty** – thirsty

his master that he saw something near the spring that looked like Mohawks (which he said were only stumps aside).[10] His master, being a most courageous warrior, went with James to make discovery. And when they came to the brow of the hill, James pointed to the stumps, and withal[11] touched his kettle with his toe, which gave it motion down the hill. And at every turn of the kettle the bail[12] clattered, upon which James and his master could see a Mohawk in every stump on motion, and turned tail to, and he was the best man that could run fastest. This alarmed all the Indians in the village. They, though about thirty or forty in number, packed off, bag and baggage, some up the river and others down, and did not return under fifteen days. And the heat of the weather being finally over, our hard service abated for this season. I never heard that the Indians understood the occasion of the fright, but James and I had many a private laugh about it.

But my most intimate and dear companion was one John Evans, a young man taken from Quochecho. We, as often as

---

[10] **aside** – in private
[11] **withal** – at the same time
[12] **bail** – handle

we could, met together and made known our grievances to each other, which seemed to ease our minds. But when it was known by the Indians, we were strictly examined apart, and falsely accused that we were contriving to desert. But we were too far from the sea to have any thought of that, and when they found our story agreed, we received no punishment.

An English captive girl about this time, who was taken by Medocawando, would often falsely accuse us of plotting to desert, but we made the truth so plainly appear, that she was checked[13] and we released.

But the third winter of my captivity he went into the country and the Indians imposed a heavy burden on him,  though he was extreme weak with long fasting. And, as he was going off the upland over a place of ice, which was very hollow, he broke through, fell down, and cut his knee very much. Notwithstanding, he traveled for some time, but the wind and cold were so forcible that they soon overcame him, and he sat or fell down, and all the Indians passed by him. Some of them went back the next day, after him or his pack, and found him, with a dog in his arms, both froze as stiff as a stake. And all my fellow-captives were dispersed and dead, but through infinite and unmerited goodness I was supported under and carried through all difficulties.

"A thousand shall fall at thy side, and ten thousand at thy right hand; but it shall not come nigh thee."
Psalm 91:7

---

[13] **checked** – rebuked

Questions for Comprehension and Discussion

1. What happened to Gyles while his master was in Canada?

2. Gyles considered killing the Indians when they gave him a tomahawk. Why did he decide not to?

3. What kept the Indians from killing Gyles?

4. What trick did James Alexander play on the Indians?

5. How did Gyles clear himself from the false charge of plotting to escape?

6. What happened to Gyles' best friend, John Evans?

7. What does this chapter of Gyles' life teach us about God?

CHAPTER FOUR

Further Difficulties and Deliverances

*"Because he hath set his love upon Me,
therefore will I deliver him: I will set him on high,
because he hath known My name."
Psalm 91:14*

One winter, as we were moving from place to place, our hunters killed some moose. And, one lying some miles from our wigwams, a young Indian and myself were ordered to fetch part of it. We set out in the morning, when the weather was promising, but it proved a very cold, cloudy day. It was late in the evening [when] we arrived at the place where the

moose lay, so that we had no time to provide materials for fire or shelter. At the same time a storm came on very thick of snow, and continued till the next morning. We made a small fire with what little rubbish we could find around us, which, with the heat of our bodies, melted the snow upon us as fast as it fell, and filled our clothes with water. Nevertheless, early in the morning

we took our loads of moose flesh and set out in order to return to our wigwams. We had not traveled far before my moose-skin coat (which was the only garment that I had on my back, and the hair was in most places worn off), was frozen stiff round my knees like a hoop, as likewise my snow-shoes and snow-clouts[1]

---
[1] **snow-clouts** – rags

to my feet! Thus I marched the whole day without fire or food! At first I was in great pain, then my flesh [became] numbed, and I felt at times extreme sick, and thought I could not travel one foot further, but wonderfully revived again.

After long traveling I felt very drowsy, and had thought of sitting down, which, had I done, without doubt I had fallen on my final sleep, as my dear companion Evans had done before. For my Indian companion, being better clothed, had left me long before. But again my spirits revived as much as if I had received the richest cordial!² Some hours after sunset I recovered³ the wigwam, and crawled in with my snow-shoes on. The Indians

---

² **cordial** – something reviving the spirit
³ **recovered** – came to

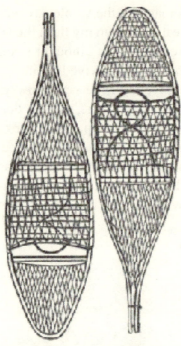

cried out, "The captive is frozen to death!"

They took off my pack, and where that lay against my back was the only place that was not frozen. The Indians cut off my shoes and stripped the clouts from my feet, which were as void of feeling as any frozen flesh could be. But I had not sat long by the fire before the blood began to circulate, and my feet to my

ankles turned black, and swelled with bloody blisters, and were inexpressibly painful. The Indians said one to another, "His feet will rot, and he'll die." Nevertheless I slept well at night. Soon after, the skin came off my feet from my ankles, whole, like a shoe, and left my toes naked without a nail, and the ends of my great toe bones bare, which in a little time turned black, so that I was obliged to cut the first joint off with my knife.

The Indians gave me rags to bind up my feet, and advised me to apply fir balsam,[4] but withal[5] said that they believed it was not worth while to use means, for I should certainly die. But, by the use of my elbows and a stick in each hand, I shoved myself on my bottom over the snow from one tree to another, till I got some fir balsam. Then [I] burned it in a clamshell till it was of a consistence like salve, and applied it to my feet and ankles and, by the divine blessing, within a week I could go about upon my heels with my staff. And, through God's goodness, we had provisions enough, so that we did not remove[6] under ten or fifteen days. And then the Indians made two little hoops, something in the form as a snowshoe, and seized[7] them to my feet, and I followed them in their track, on my heels, from place to place, sometimes half leg deep in snow and water, which gave me the most acute pain imaginable, but I was forced to walk

[4] **balsam** – resin or sap

[5] **withal** – at the same time

[6] **remove** – move

[7] **seized** – tied

or die. But within a year my feet were entirely well, and the nails came on my great toes, so that a very critical eye could scarce perceive any part missing, or that they had been frozen at all!

> *"Because he hath set his love upon Me,*
> *therefore will I deliver him: I will set him on high,*
> *because he hath known My name."*
> *Psalm 91:14*

Questions for Comprehension and Discussion

1. What happened to Gyles during the winter moose-hunting?

2. How did the Indians respond to Gyles' frostbite?

3. How did Gyles respond to the frostbite?

4. 2 Chronicles 16:9 reads: "For the eyes of the LORD run to and fro throughout the whole earth, to shew Himself strong in the behalf of them whose heart is perfect toward Him." How did the Lord show Himself strong on Gyles' behalf?

5. What does Psalm 91:14 give as the reasons why God delivers His own?

CHAPTER FIVE

The Lord's Protecting Me from Harm

"Because thou hast made the Lord, *which is my refuge,
even the most High, thy habitation;
There shall no evil befall thee,
neither shall any plague come nigh thy dwelling."
Psalm 91:9–10*

In a time of great scarcity of provisions the Indians chased a large moose into the river and killed him. And [they] brought the flesh to the village and laid it on a scaffold in a large wigwam, in order to make a feast. I was very officious[1] in supplying them with wood and water, which pleased them so well that they now and then gave me a piece of flesh half boiled or roasted, which I did eat with eagerness, and I doubt without great thankfulness to the divine Being who so extraordinarily fed me! At length the scaffold broke, and one large piece fell and knocked me on the head. (The Indians said that I lay stunned a considerable time.) The first [thing] I was sensible of was a murmuring noise in my ears, then my sight gradually returned, with an extreme pain in my head (which was very much bruised) and it was long before I recovered, the weather being very hot.

---

[1] **officious** – obliging

I was once with an Indian fishing for sturgeon[2] [and,] the Indian darting[3] one, his feet slipped, and turned the canoe bottom upwards with me under it holding fast [to] the cross-bar (for I could not swim) with my face to the bottom of the canoe, but I turned myself and brought my breast to bear on the cross-bar, expecting every minute that the Indian would have towed me to the bank. But he had other fish to fry! Thus I continued a quarter of an hour, without want of breath, sounding for bottom till the current drove me on a rocky point where I could reach bottom. There I stopped and turned up my canoe. I looked for the Indian, and he was half a mile distant up the river. I went to him, and asked, why he did not tow me to the bank, seeing he knew that I could not swim? He said he knew that I was under the canoe, for there were no bubbles any where to be seen, and that, [being driven by the current,] I should drive on the point. Therefore he took care of his fine sturgeon, which was eight or ten feet long.

While at the Indian village, I had been cutting wood and was binding it up with an Indian rope in order to carry it to the wigwam, when a stout, ill-natured young fellow, about twenty

---

[2] **sturgeon** – a fish growing from 7 to 12 feet long
[3] **darting** – spearing

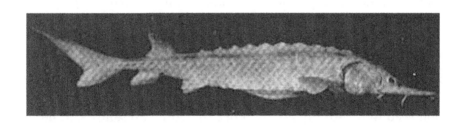

years of age, threw me backward, sat on my chest, and pulling out his knife, said that he would kill me, for he had never yet killed an English person. I told him that he might go to war, and that would be more manly than to kill a poor captive who was doing their drudgery for them. Notwithstanding all that I could say, he began to cut and stab me on my breast. I seized him by the hair, and tumbling him from off me on his back, and followed him with my fist and knee so that he presently said he had enough. But when I saw the blood run and felt the smart, I [was] at him again, and bid him get up and not lie there like a dog. [I] told him of his former abuses offered to me and other poor captives, and that if ever he offered the like to me again, I would pay him double. I sent him before me, took up my burden of wood, and came to the Indians and told them the whole truth, and they commended me. And I don't remember that ever he offered me the least abuse afterward, though he was big enough to have dispatched[4] two of me.

---

[4] **dispatched** – killed

I pray God I may never be forgetful of his wonderful goodness! And [I pray] that these instances may excite others in their adversities to make their addresses[5] to the Almighty and put their confidence in Him in the use of proper means.

> *"Because thou hast made the* Lord, *which is my refuge,*
> *even the most High, thy habitation;*
> *There shall no evil befall thee,*
> *neither shall any plague come nigh thy dwelling."*
> *Psalm 91:9-10*

---

[5] **addresses** – petitions

Questions for Comprehension and Discussion

1. List the Lord's protection of Gyles after the Indians had brought in a moose.

2. Describe Gyles' encounter with the young Indian fellow.

3. This Indian encounter caused Gyles to pray that he might never forget something. What was it that he did not wish to forget?

4. How forgetful are we of the goodness and mercy of God in our own lives?

CHAPTER SIX

The Indians Calling upon the Devil

"Thou shalt not be afraid for the terror by night; nor for the arrow that flieth by day."
Psalm 91:5

The Indians are very often surprised with the appearance of ghosts and demons, and sometimes encouraged by the Devil, for they go to him for success in hunting, etc. I was once hunting with Indians who were not brought over to the Romish Faith,[1] and after several days' hunting they proposed to inquire, according to their custom, what success they should have. They accordingly prepared many hot stones and laid them in a heap, and made a small hut covered with skins and mats. And then in the dark night two of the powwows[2] went into this hot-house with a large vessel of water, which at times they poured on those hot rocks, which raised a thick steam, so that a third Indian gave it vent when they were almost

---
[1] **Romish Faith** – Roman Catholic religion
[2] **powwows** – *i.e.*, Indians

suffocated.

There was an old squaw who was kind to captives, and never joined with them in their powwowing,³ to whom I manifested an earnest desire to see their management. She told me that if they knew of my being there they would kill me, and that when she was a girl she had known young persons to be taken away by an hairy man, and therefore she would not advise me to go, lest the hairy man should carry me away. I told her that I was not afraid of the hairy man, nor could he hurt me if she would not discover⁴ me to the powwows. At length she promised that she would not, but charged me to be careful of myself.

I went within three or four feet of the hot-house, for it was very dark, and heard strange noises and yelling, such as I never heard before.

---

³ **powwowing** – pagan ritual

⁴ **discover** – reveal

At times the Indian who tended without would lift up the mat and a steam rise up which looked like fire in the dark. I lay there two or three hours, but saw none of their hairy men or demons. And when I found that they had finished their ceremony, I went to the wigwam and told the squaw what had passed, who was glad
that I returned without hurt, and never discovered[5] what I had done. After some time inquiry was made what success we were like to have in our hunting. The powwows said that they had very likely signs of success, but no real visible appearance as at other times. A few days after we moved up the river and had pretty good success.

One afternoon as I was in a canoe with one of the powwows, the dog barked, and presently a moose passed by within a few rods of us, so that the waves which he made by wading rolled our canoe. The Indian shot at him, but the moose took very little notice of it, and went into the woods to the southward. The fellow said, "I'll try if I can't fetch you back

---

[5] **discovered** – revealed

for all your haste." The evening following we built our two wigwams on a sandy point on the upper end of an island in the river, northwest of the place where the moose went into the woods, and the Indian powwowed the greatest part of the night following. And in the morning we had the fair track of a moose round our wigwams, though we did not see or taste of it. I am of opinion that the devil was permitted to humor those unhappy wretches sometimes in some things.

When the Indians determine for war, or are entering upon a particular expedition, they kill a number of their dogs, burn off their hair, and cut them into pieces, leaving only one dog's head whole. The rest of the flesh they boil and make a fine feast of it. After which the dog's head that was left whole is scorched till the nose and lips have shrunk from the teeth and left them bare and grinning. This done, they fasten it on a stick, and the Indian who is proposed to be chief in the expedition takes the head into his hand and sings a warlike song, in which he mentions the town they design to attack, and the principal man in it, threatening that in a few days he will carry that man's head and scalp in his hand in the same manner. When the chief hath sung, he so places the dog's head as to grin at him whom he supposeth will go his second, who, if he accepts, takes the head in his hand and sings; but if he refuse to go he turns the teeth to another; and thus from one to another till they have enlisted their company.

The Indians imagine that dog's flesh makes them bold and courageous! I have seen an Indian split a dog's head with a hatchet, and take out the brains hot, and eat them raw with the blood running down his jaws!

"Thou shalt not be afraid for the terror by night;
nor for the arrow that flieth by day."
Psalm 91:5

Questions for Comprehension and Discussion

1. How did the Indians seek to see into the future?

2. Explain Biblically why the Indians were wrong in what they did.

3. Though the Indians called upon the devil, was he able to grant their request?

4. In what ways do we seek answers today from sources other than God's Word?

CHAPTER SEVEN

Sold to the French

*"For He shall give His angels charge over thee,
to keep thee in all thy ways."
Psalm 91:11*

When about six years of my doleful captivity had passed, my second Indian master died, whose squaw and my first Indian master disputed whose slave I should be. And some malicious persons advised them to end the quarrel by putting a period to my life. But honest Father Simon, the priest of the river, told them that it would be a heinous crime, and advised them to sell me to the French.

There came annually one or two men-of-war[1] to supply the fort, which was on the river about thirty-four leagues from the sea. The Indians having advice of the arrival of a man-of-war at the mouth of the river, they, about thirty or forty in number, went aboard: for the gentlemen from France made a present to them every year, and set forth the riches and victories of

---
[1] **men-of-war** – war ships

their monarch, etc.

At this time they presented a bag or two of flour with some prunes as ingredients for a feast. I, who was dressed up in an old greasy blanket, without cap, hat, or shirt (for I had no shirt for the six years but that which was on my back when I was taken), was invited into the great cabin where many well-rigged[2] gentlemen were sitting, who would fain[3] have had a full view of me. I endeavored to hide myself behind the hangings, for I was much ashamed, thinking of my former wearing clothes, and of my living with people who could rig[4] as well as the best of them.

My [former] master asked me whether I chose to be sold aboard the man-of-war or to the inhabitants. I replied with tears, "I should be glad if you would sell me to the English from whom you took me. But if I must be sold to the French, I choose to be sold to the lowest on the river, or nearest inhabitants to the sea," about twenty-five leagues from the mouth of the river. For I thought that if I were sold to the gentlemen aboard the man of war I should never return to the English. This was the first sight I had of saltwater in my captivity, and the first time that I had tasted salt or bread.

---
[2] **rigged** – dressed
[3] **fain** – gladly
[4] **rig** – dress

My master presently went ashore, and after a few days all the Indians went up the river. And, when we came to the house which I mentioned to my master, he went ashore with me and tarried all night. The master of the house spake kindly to me in Indian, for I could not then speak one word of French. Madam also looked pleasant on me and gave me some bread. The next day I was sent six leagues further up the river to another French house. My master and the friar tarried with Monsieur Decbouffour, the gentleman who had entertained us the night before. Not long after, Father Simon came and said, "Now you are one of us, for you are sold to that gentleman by whom you were entertained the other night." I replied. "Sold! to a Frenchman!" I could say no more, went into the woods alone, and wept till I could scarce see or stand! The word sold, and that to a people of that persuasion which my dear mother so much detested, and in her last words manifested so great fears of my falling into! The thoughts of these almost broke my heart!

When I had given vent to my passions,[5] I rubbed my eyes, endeavoring to hide my grief, but Father Simon, perceiving that my eyes were swollen, called me aside and bid me not to grieve, for the gentleman to whom I was sold was of a good humor,[6] that he had formerly bought two captives of the Indians, who both went home to Boston. This in some measure revived

---

[5] **passions** – emotions

[6] **humor** – disposition

me. But he added that he did not suppose that I would ever incline to go to the English, for the French way of worship was much to be preferred: also that he should pass that way in about ten days, and if I did not like to live with the French better than with the Indians, he would buy me again.

On the day following, Father Simon and my Indian master went up the river six and thirty leagues to their chief village, and I went down the river six leagues with two Frenchmen to my new master, who kindly received me. And in a few days Madam made me an Osnaburg[7] shirt and French cap, and a coat out of one of my master's old coats. Then I threw away my greasy blanket and Indian flap.

And I never more saw the old friar, the Indian village, or my Indian master (till about fourteen years after I saw my Indian master at Port Royal whither I was sent by the government with a flag of truce, for exchanging prisoners, and again about twenty-four years' since he came from St. John's to George's to see me, where I made him very welcome).

My French master held a great trade with the Indians, which suited me very well, I being thorough in the languages of the tribes at Cape Sable's and St. John's. I had not lived long with this gentleman before he committed to me the keys of his store, etc. And my whole employment was trading and hunting,

---

[7] **Osnaburg** – course German linen

in which I acted faithfully for my master, and never knowingly wronged him to the value of one farthing.

They spake to me so frequently in Indian that it was some time before I was perfect in the French tongue. Monsieur generally had his goods from the man-of-war which came there annually from France.

In the year 1696 two men-of-war came to the mouth of the river. They made the Indians some presents and invited them to join in an expedition to Pemaquid, which invitation they accepted and soon after arrived there. And Captain Chubb delivered the fort without much dispute to Monsieur D'Iberville their chief, as I heard the gentleman say whom I lived with, who was there present.

Monsieur D'Iberville

Early in the spring I was sent with three Frenchmen to the mouth of the river for provision which came from Port Royal. We carried[8] over land from the river to a large bay, where we were driven on an island by a northeast storm, and were kept there seven days without any sustenance, for we expected a quick passage and carried nothing with us. The wind continued boisterous so that we could not return back, and the ice prevented our going forward.

After seven days the ice broke up and we went forward, though we were so weak that we could scarce hear each other speak. And the people at the mouth of the river were surprised to see us so feeble, and advised us to be cautious and abstemious[9] in eating. By this time I knew as much of fasting as they, and

---

[8] **carried** – transported boats or canoes

[9] **abstemious** – moderate, sparing

dieted on broth and recovered very well, as also one of the others did. But the other two would not be advised, and I never saw any person in greater torment than they were, till they obtained a passage, on which they recovered.

> *"For He shall give His angels charge over thee,*
> *to keep thee in all thy ways."*
> Psalm 91:11

Questions for Comprehension and Discussion

1. Why did Gyles not wish to be sold to the French?

2. How did Gyles seek to honor his mother?

3. Twenty-four years after being sold to the French, Gyles again met his Indian master. How did he treat him? List some Scriptures that might have motivated Gyles to this action.

4. Gyles' French master entrusted him with his store, etc. How did Gyles handle this charge? Why?

CHAPTER EIGHT

My Trial with False Religion

*"He shall cover thee with His feathers,
and under His wings shalt thou trust:
His truth shall be thy shield and buckler."*
Psalm 91:4

A friar who lived in the family invited me to confession, but I excused myself as well as I could. One evening he took me into his apartment in the dark and advised me to confess to him what sins I had committed. I told him that I could not remember a thousandth part of them, they were so numerous. Then he bid me remember and relate as many as I could and he would pardon them, signifying that he had a bag to put them in. I told him that I did not believe that it was in the power of any but God to pardon sin. He asked me whether I had read the Bible. I told him that I had when I was a little boy, so long since that

I had forgotten most of it. Then he told me that he did not pardon my sins, but when he knew them he prayed God to pardon them. He wished me well, and hoped that I should be better advised, and said that he should call for me in a little time. Thus he dismissed [me], and never called me to confession more.

The gentleman whom I lived with had a fine field of wheat, which great numbers of blackbirds visited and destroyed much of. But the French said a Jesuit would come and banish them. [He] came at length and all things were prepared, viz.,[1] a basin of what they call holy water, a staff with a little brush to sprinkle withal,[2] and the Jesuit's white robe, which he put on. (I asked several prisoners who had lately been taken by privateers[3] and brought hither, viz., Mr. Woodberry, Cocks, and Morgan, whether they would go and see the ceremony? Mr. Woodberry asked me whether I designed to go. I told him that I did. He said that I was then as bad a Papist[4] as they, and a —— fool. I told him that I believed as little of it as they did, but I inclined to

---

[1] **viz.** – that is, namely
[2] **withal** – with
[3] **privateers** – armed sea vessels employed during wartime
[4] **Papist** – Roman Catholic

see the ceremony, that I might rehearse[5] it to the English.)

They entered the field and walked through the wheat in procession, a young lad going before the Jesuit with a basin of their holy water, then the Jesuit, with his brush dipping it into the basin, and sprinkling the field on each side of him. Next him a little bell tingling and about thirty men following in order, singing with the Jesuit, "Ora pro Nobis."[6] At the end of the field they wheeled to the left about, and returned. Thus they went through the field of wheat, the birds rising before them and lighting[7] behind them.

At their return I said to a French lad, "The friar hath done no service. He had better take a gun and shoot the birds." The lad left me a while (I thought, to ask the Jesuit what to say), and when he returned he said the sins of the people were so great that the friar could not prevail against those creatures. The same Jesuit as vainly attempted to banish the mosquitoes at Sigenecto, for the sins of that people were so great also that he could not prevail against them, but rather drew more, as the French informed me!

> *"He shall cover thee with His feathers,*
> *and under His wings shalt thou trust:*
> *His truth shall be thy shield and buckler."*
> *Psalm 91:4*

---

[5] **rehearse** – recount
[6] **Ora pro Nobis** – Pray for us
[7] **lighting** – landing

Questions for Comprehension and Discussion

1. As a young child Gyles' parents taught him the Scriptures. How did this change how Gyles responded to his captors and those he met during his captivity?

2. What did the friar ask Gyles to do? How did Gyles respond?

3. What is the only way that sins can be forgiven?

3. What does Psalm 91:4 declare God's truth to be?

4. List some ways that your family could study Scripture in order to be better equipped for the situations that meet you.

CHAPTER NINE

God's Mercy in Returning Me to the English

"With long life will I satisfy him, and shew Him my salvation."
Psalm 91:16

Some time after, Colonel Hawthorn attempted the taking the French fort up this river. We heard of them some time before they came up the river by the guard that Governor Villebon had ordered at the river's mouth. Monsieur, the gentleman whom I lived with, was gone to France, and Madam advised with me. She then desired me to nail the paper on the door of our house, containing as follows:

> I entreat the General of the English not to burn

my house, or barn, nor destroy my cattle. I don't suppose that such an army [has] come up this river to destroy a few inhabitants, but for the fort above us. I have shown kindness to the English captives, as we were capacitated,[1] and have bought two captives of the Indians, and sent them to Boston: and have one now with us, and he shall go also when a convenient opportunity presents, and he desires it.

This done, Madam said to me: "Little English, we have shown you kindness, and now it lies in your power to serve or disserve us, as you know where our goods are hid in the woods, and that Monsieur is not at home. I could have sent you to the fort and put you under confinement, but my respects to you and assurance of your love to us has disposed me to confide in you, persuaded that you will not hurt us nor our affairs. And now if you will not run away to the English who are coming up the river, but serve our interest, I will acquaint Monsieur of it at his return from France, which will be very pleasing to him. And I now give my word that you shall have liberty to go to Boston on the first opportunity (if you desire it), or that any other favor in my power shall not be denied you."

I replied, "Madam, it is contrary to the nature of the

---

[1] **capacitated** – able

English to requite[2] evil for good. I shall endeavor to serve you and your interest. I shall not run to the English, but if I am taken by them, shall willingly go with them, and yet endeavor not to disserve you, either in your persons or goods."

This said, we embarked and went in a large boat and canoe two or three miles up an eastern branch of the river that comes from a large pond, and in the evening sent down four hands to make discovery. And while they were sitting in the house, the English surrounded it and took one of the four. The other three made their escape in the dark through the English soldiers, and came to us, and gave a surprising account of affairs. Again Madam said to me, "Little English, now you can go from us, but I hope you will remember your word!" I said, "Madam, be not concerned, for I will not leave you in this strait."[3] She said, "I know not what to do with my two poor little babes!" I said, "Madam, the sooner we embark and go over the great pond the better."

Accordingly we embarked and went over the pond. The next day we spake with Indians who were in a canoe, and gave us an account that Sigenecto town was taken and burnt. Soon

---

[2] **requite** – repay
[3] **strait** – difficulty

after we heard the great guns at Governor Villebon's fort, which the English engaged several days, killed one man, and drew off and went down the river, for it was so late in the fall that, had they tarried a few days longer in the river, they would have been frozen in for the winter.

Hearing no report of the great guns for several days, I, with two others, went down to our house to make discovery, where we found our young lad who was taken by the English when they went up the river, for the General [Benjamin Church] was so honorable that, on reading the note on our door, he ordered that the house and barn should not be burnt, nor their cattle or other creatures killed, except one or two, and the poultry for their use. And at their return [he] ordered the young lad to be put ashore. Finding things in this posture, we returned and gave Madam an account.

She acknowledged the many favors which the English had shewn her with gratitude, and treated me with great civility. The next spring Monsieur arrived from France in the man-of-war, who thanked me for my care of his affairs, and said that he would endeavor to fulfill what Madam had promised me.

And accordingly, in the year 1698, the peace being proclaimed and a sloop come to the mouth of the river with a ransom for one Michael Cooms, I put Monsieur in mind[4] of his word. I told him that there was now an opportunity for me

---

[4] **mind** – remembrance

to go and see the English. He advised me to tarry, and told me that he would do for me as for his own, etc. I thanked him for his kindness, but chose rather to go to Boston, for I hoped that I had some relations[5] yet alive. Then he advised me to go up to the fort and take my leave of the governor, which I did, and he spake very kindly, etc.

Some days after I took my leave of Madam, Monsieur went down to the mouth of the river with me to see me safe aboard, and asked the master, Mr. Starkes, a Scotchman, whether I must pay for my passage. If so, he would pay it himself rather than I should have it to pay at my arrival at Boston, but gave me not a penny. The master told him that there was nothing to pay and that if the owner should make any demand, he would pay it himself, rather than a poor prisoner should suffer, for he was glad to see any English person come out of captivity.

On the thirteenth of June I took my leave of Monsieur, and the sloop came to sail for Boston, where we arrived on the nineteenth of the same, at night. In the morning after my arrival

[5] **relations** – relatives

a youth came on board and asked many questions relating to my captivity, and at length gave me to understand that he was my little brother who was at play with some other children, and upon hearing the guns and seeing the Indians run, made their escape to the fort and went off with the captain and people. And [he told me] that my elder brother, who made his escape from the farm whence I was taken, and our two little sisters, were alive, and that our mother had been dead some years, etc. (as above related). Then we went ashore and saw our elder brother, etc.

On the second of August, 1689, I was taken, and on the nineteenth of June, 1698, arrived at Boston, so that I was absent eight years, ten months, and seventeen days. In all which time, though I underwent extreme difficulties, yet I saw much of the goodness of God.

May the most powerful and beneficent[6] Being accept of this public testimony of it, and bless my experiences to excite[7] others to confide in His All-sufficiency, through the infinite merits of Jesus Christ!

---

[6] **beneficent** – good

[7] **excite** – stir up, rouse

*"With long life will I satisfy him,
and shew Him my salvation."*
Psalm 91:16

Questions for Comprehension and Discussion

1. When Benjamin Church sailed up the river to take the French fort, what did Gyles' captor ask of him?

2. How did Gyles respond to Madam's request?

3. Why didn't Gyles run away when he had the chance to escape to the English?

4. How did the English respond to Madam's note?

5. What did Gyles' master do when he returned from France?

6. Who met Gyles on his return to Boston?

7. What was Gyles' response to his years of captivity?

These private memoirs were collected from my minutes, at the earnest request of my second consort,[1] for the use of our family, that we might have a memento[2] ever ready at hand, to excite in ourselves gratitude and thankfulness to God; and in our offspring a due sense of their dependence on the Sovereign of the universe, from the precariousness[3] and vicissitudes[4] of all sublunary[5] enjoyments. In this state, and for this end, they have laid by me for some years.

— John Gyles Esq. 1736

In October of 1698, just four months after his return, John Gyles was employed by Lieutenant Governor Stoughton to act as interpreter for two officers sent to exchange prisoners with the Indians. Gyles' fluency in several Indian dialects and his excellent French made him invaluable in the difficult task of trying to reclaim the English taken by the Indians. For over ten years the civil government called on his knowledge of languages to aid in prisoner exchanges, criminal trials involving Indians, and acting as private interpreter. He had the satisfaction to see how his years in captivity prepared him for a role to bring others out of the terrors and captivities of the Indians and restore them to their own families and homes.

---

[1] **consort** – wife
[2] **memento** – reminder
[3] **precariousness** – uncertainty
[4] **vicissitudes** – change
[5] **sublunary** – earthly

Here I raise mine Ebenezer,
hither by Thy help I'm come;
and I hope, by Thy good pleasure,
safely to arrive at home.
Jesus sought me when a stranger,
wand'ring from the fold of God;
He to rescue me from danger,
interposed His precious blood.

O to grace how great a debtor
daily I'm constrained to be!
Let Thy goodness, like a fetter,
bind my wand'ring heart to Thee.
Prone to wander, Lord, I feel it,
prone to leave the God I love;
Here's my heart, O take and seal it,
seal it for Thy courts above.

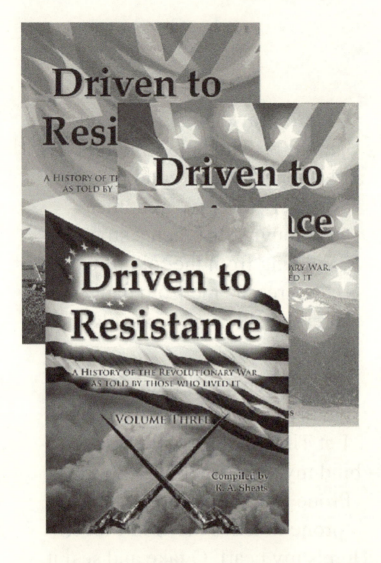

"Do you want a usable and enjoyable book to teach your children about the founding of the American Republic? Here it is."

— William Potter

Historian, *The American History Guild* **and** *Landmark Events*

If you enjoyed *In Him Will I Trust,*
you may also enjoy:

Driven to Resistance

A HISTORY OF THE REVOLUTIONARY WAR AS TOLD BY THOSE LIVED IT

The year is 1765. George Washington, a colonel from Virginia, is thirty-three years old. Thomas Jefferson, a young law student in Williamsburg, has just passed his twenty-first year. British America is alive with the effects of the Great Awakening, and across the Atlantic the Parliament of Britain is busy determining the proper method of taxing the American colonies.

1765 is the year, and history is about to be made. Join Washington, John Adams, Patrick Henry, and their contemporaries as they chronicle the events of their lives, recounting in their own words the acts and aggressions of Parliament and their own part in the struggle for liberty known as the American War for Independence.

Driven to Resistance recounts the history of the Revolutionary War by the republication of the original writings of the time. Chronologically ordered and copiously illustrated, *Driven to Resistance* offers the modern reader easy and understandable access to the documents and diaries of our eighteenth-century forefathers. From the writings of Washington to the debates of Parliament, the reader is presented with original documents rendered easily-accessible to the contemporary reader.

Without a Home or Country

A Gallant Tale of the Last Stand of the Confederacy

by Cornelius Hunt, One of her Officers

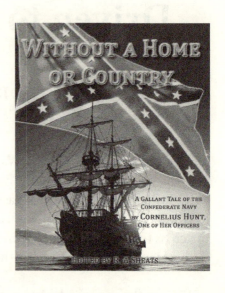

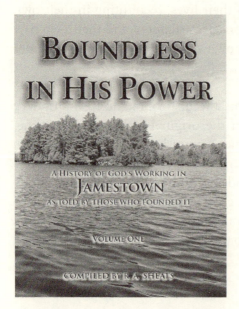

Boundless in His Power

A History of God's Working in Jamestown, as told by those who founded it

JOHN PATON
FOR YOUNG FOLKS

The classic Autobiography
of Missionary
John G. Paton

*Makes a great
family read-aloud!*

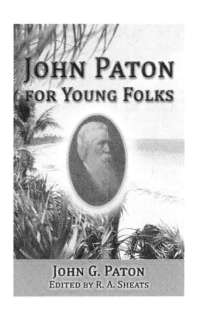

PIRATES, PURITANS,
AND THE PERILS
OF THE HIGH SEAS

The True History
of Pirates, written by
Those who Knew Them

*For a complete listing of available titles, please visit:
www.psalm78ministries.com*

Daybreak in Alaska

Sheldon Jackson
and the Gospel's Entrance
into the Wild West
and Alaska

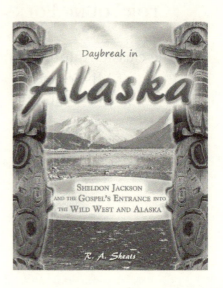

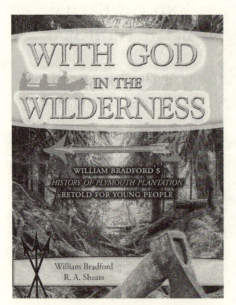

With God in the Wilderness

*William Bradford's
History of Plymouth
Plantation
retold for young people*

Made in the USA
Las Vegas, NV
29 September 2024